Fair View – Childhood Memories of a Magical Place

"In loving memory of my niece Anne Madden (neé Peacock) (1953–1990) who rests in peace in South Africa."

Fair View –
Childhood Memories
of a Magical Place

Mary S. Peacock

SDH Publishing
2009

First published 2009
by
SDH Publishing
Chaucer House, Mill Lane, Othery, Bridgwater, Somerset TA7 0QT

ISBN 978-0-9561400-1-2

Other titles by Mary S. Peacock

Grandfather's Samplers and the Peacock Tree. 2001. Romsey, Hampshire, Village and Family History Project. ISBN 1-903979-00-5 (reprinted 2009 by SDH Publishing).

Pinkneys Green – A History. 2009. Othery, Somerset, SDH Publishing. ISBN 978-0-9561400-2-9

Acknowledgement
My grateful thanks to Mrs Tina Skinner who skillfully
processed the initial drafts of my books.

Printed by
CPI Antony Rowe, Chippenham, Wiltshire

Contents

Introduction

This is the story of us young Peacocks,[1] eventually five of us, who from 1913 grew up in a house called Fair View, Kent's Corner, Pinkneys Green, near Maidenhead – in those days a house with no electricity, gas, hot water, main drainage or telephone. Outside the front gate were the common lands of Pinkneys Green and Maidenhead Thicket, the only playgrounds we ever needed. Villagers had Commoners' rights. The local dairy herd, accompanied by a cowman, freely grazed the whole area, together with horses, geese, ducks and chicken. We children came to know every inch of this vast acreage of commons and woodlands with all its ancient quarries and pits, with many ponds. Flowers, mostly chalk-lovers, abounded. The quickthorn and mature trees towards Stubbings were havens for countless birds.

Our nearest route to Maidenhead was on foot, over the stile by our front gate at Kent's Corner, then across farm footpaths as far as the edge of Maidenhead Borough, about a mile and a half. This was our way to Alwyn Road School.

Then everything changed. The farmland between us and Maidenhead was sold off in building plots. In 1920 planning permission was granted for the first houses to be built along the footpath route. Thus, Pinkneys Road came into being.

It soon became obvious that in all but name we were part of Maidenhead and in 1934, following the review of County boundaries under the Local Government Act 1929, Pinkneys Green Commons, Maidenhead Thicket, along with Furze Platt and Bray, became part of the Borough of Maidenhead.

[1] Details of the Peacock family can be found in Peacock, Mary S. *Grandfather's Samplers and the Peacock Tree* (2001; 2009).

1

In the same year the National Trust acquired the manorial rights over the Commons.

Then came World War II. Sixty-four acres of the open area of the Commons were ploughed for food production, notwithstanding the fact that over the centuries Pinkneys Green had been designated "manor waste, non-cultivable for any useful purpose". Although the area was de-requisitioned in 1962, to this day it is still managed as it could never be left to regenerate. With grazing no longer possible, the Commons produce only coarse grass which needs mowing annually.

Our magical place was gone forever.

As I began to collect old photographs and maps of Pinkneys Green, I realised that I knew little of the history of this ancient manor. There are a few published accounts, notably in Luke Over's work on Maidenhead (1984) and Cookham (1994), in the Victoria County History, Berkshire (1972), and from the National Trust (1979). There came to my notice the volumes of notes of one Stephen Darby, Cookham historian, who, around 1900, meticulously researched all early national archives relating to Cookham, including references to Pinkneys Green and the Thicket (1899; 1909).

From the 1890s until 1934 Pinkneys Green and the Thicket were administered by Cookham Rural District Council. They held their first meeting in January 1895. Their Minutes (1895–1934), held by Berkshire Record Office in Reading, have been searched for mentions of Pinkneys Green that are included in my notes on research into the history of Pinkneys Green and Maidenhead Thicket, and recorded in a separate document.[2]

[2] Peacock, Mary S. *Pinkneys Green – A History*. Othery, Somerset, SDH Publishing, 2009.

Early Memories

I was born at Mossy Bank, Courthouse Road, Furze Platt, Cookham Rural District, near Maidenhead on 5 June 1911. My parents, George Luther Peacock and Elsie Maud Robson (a milliner), had married in London in 1910. Father was an auditor on the staff of the Great Western Railway (GWR) Audit Office at Paddington Station and on moving to Maidenhead travelled daily by train to London.

Of Mossy Bank I have only vague memories – a large black-leaded kitchen range with a very high (or so it seemed to me) mantelpiece with the old kitchen clock which became part of all our later lives. And over the side path an archway of lovely climbing roses, shading the pram. Next door there was a very kind lady called Mrs Dorsett.

I have no recollection of the occasion of the studio photo (below) taken in Tenby. Grandma Robson (neé Pond) had a brother in Tenby and the great-grandparents, the Rhind

Mary Sheila Peacock

Ponds, lived in Mumbles, so we must have been visiting. The bonnet was to hide my total lack of hair, so I was told!

My sister, Joan Kathleen Peacock, was born at Mossy Bank on 30 January 1913. Meanwhile father was negotiating to buy the house he had set his heart on – Fair View, Kents Corner, Pinkneys Green.

Pinkneys Green (map SU 860825), together with Maidenhead Thicket, formed the southern boundary of Cookham Manor. Once part of Windsor Forest, the Manor was held by the Crown until 1818. Thereafter the manorial rights were acquired by different Lords of the Manor until 1934 when the National Trust acquired the rights over the Commons and Thickets for all time.

The 1931 map opposite (scale 6" to 1 mile), outlines all the many tracks and footpaths, chalk pits and quarries on Pinkneys Green and the Thicket that were so well known to the villagers. Until the building development on the Maidenhead side in the 1920s and the ploughing of much of the Commons in 1939, this area could well have looked much the same throughout the centuries.

The name 'Pinkneys' originates from that of a Norman Knight, Ghuilo de Pinkney (from Picquigney in Normandy), who fought valiantly at the Battle of Hastings and was rewarded by the Conqueror with several estates throughout the realm including the Manor of Cookham of which Pinkneys Green and Maidenhead Thicket were a part.

Over the centuries Pinkneys Green was categorised as 'manor waste', that is, it served no useful agricultural purpose. Tenants had rights – "housebote, haybote, fuel with common pasture for all animals". To keep livestock from straying onto surrounding farmland the Common was earlier gated – thus Jimmet's Gate at Pinkneys Farm, Hutton's Gate on the Bisham Meadow Road, Butler's Gate separating Pinkneys Green from Bigfrill and Kent's Corner Gate, the latter existing until 1920.

The 1899 Ordnance Survey. map shows Kent's Corner

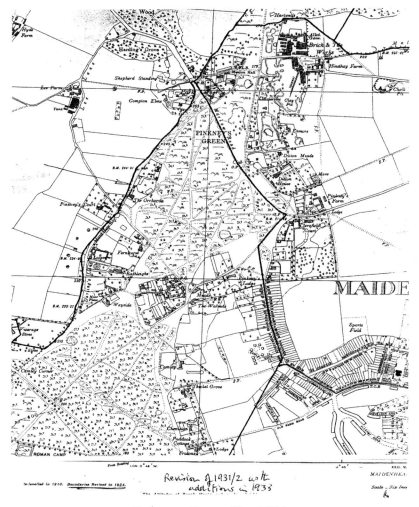

Ordnance Survey Map 1931

with a row of five Walnut Tree Cottages facing south towards the open fields. These dwellings were condemned as unfit for human habitation and demolished in 1895. Fair View was eventually built on the vacated plot.

The water supply came from wells, clearly marked on the 1899 map. Mains water did not reach the area until 1901. Drainage was into cesspits until well into the 1930s.

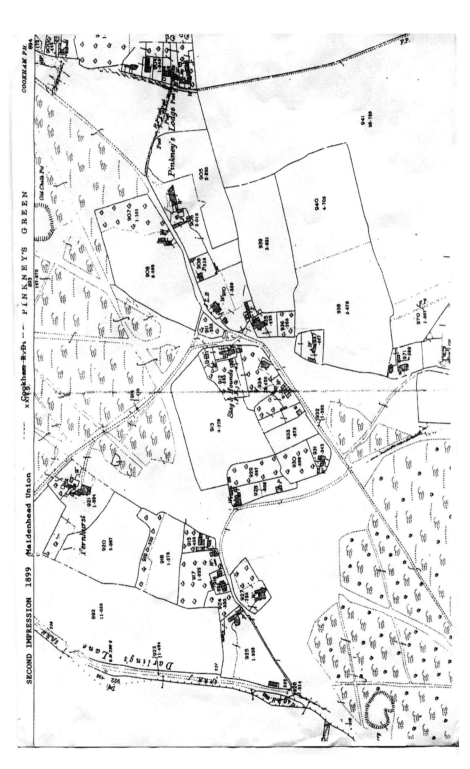

Ordance Survey map of Pinkneys Green 1899

6

The following early photos of Kent's Corner give some idea of that lovely place. The row of black poplars bounding the farm track must have been planted by an earlier Lord of the Manor. A fast-growing tree, whose wood is used for making matches, matchboxes, trug baskets and, in The Netherlands, clogs. I remember in early spring the wonderful scent of resin from the emerging buds and later in May/June the ground carpeted with white fluff fallen with the seeds from the female trees.

There must have been many a trip between Furze Platt and Kent's Corner before the move into Fair View. I, in my pushchair, was fascinated by the singing of the wind in the telegraph wires as we wended our way across the footpath towards Pinkneys Farm. Ray Knibbs (1989), writing about his schooldays in *Furze Platt Remembered* said of those singing wires:

Kent's Corner with black poplars and ponies grazing the Common

Fair View seen from Kent's Corner Gate that survived until 1920

"There was a trunk line of overhead telephone (or telegraph) wires on tall poles that went across the field by the footpath to Pinkneys Farm where Oaken Grove is today. There were more than a hundred lines, and at certain times they would make a very loud hum and the noise could be heard a great distance away"

From Pinkneys Farm we skirted Clarefield, thought to have been the site of the medieval manor house, along a farm track, past Tweed Cottage, Quernes, Fern Cottages, Furze Cottage, Town Hall Cottages, the Waggon & Horses, Walnut Tree Cottage, then ahead a farm gate and a stile and Fair View in the corner.

In those days the Waggon & Horses was just a small tap-room jutting from the main house. The brewers were H Hewett & Co. of White Waltham, and the landlord was Walter ('Wally') Piercey.

Fair View, one of a pair of semi-detached villas was built for Mr ET Biggs, founder of the jewellers business in Maidenhead. Plans for the two new houses had been approved by Cookham Rural District Council in September 1907. Mr Biggs never lived in Fair View and transferred the

The Waggon & Horses

property to his daughter, Mrs Hilda Mary Hawker, wife of RH Hawker, corn chandlers of Hart Street, Henley-on-Thames. Mrs Hawker sold both Fair View and its pair, Ashton Cottage to Mr EC Norris of 15 Sussex Street, Pimlico, a long-standing friend of my parents. Father raised a mortgage for Fair View and Ashton Cottage was let to a Mr Bloomfield.

Life at Fair View

Then at last in 1913 we moved into Fair View – this house which, for 76 years, was to be the home of several generations of the Peacock family. I well remember the excitement of jumping up and down on the bare boards in the drawing-room. It was such a lovely noise. Yes, it was the 'drawing-room', not the 'lounge' nor the 'sitting–room', but later it became just 'the front room'. Its large bay window, looked west out onto the Common and on the south side were French doors. I think it was many years before this room was carpeted – eventually the floor was covered with a lovely dull blue felt, mother's colour. A small hall space at the bottom of the stairs opened into the dining room. This had a large window facing south, an open grate with hobs either side, a built-in 'china' cupboard and a large cupboard under the stairs for brooms, brushes and things. As the

Fair View, Kent's Corner, Pinkneys Green

door had a catch on the outside on occasion one found oneself locked in! Later the doors were removed from this cupboard to make room for a wooden form to seat more children round the table. Also, in the corner, high up under the ceiling there was a little built-in cupboard, supposedly out of reach of children. The old dining room table and chairs took a lot of punishment from us children. In the kitchen was the cooking range with, over-head, a long bamboo clothes rack on pulleys and a walk-in larder, unfortunately on the south side so not very cool. The herringbone wood block floor was regularly scrubbed. Then a step down led into the scullery with sink and cold water tap. Here too was a pump drawing water from a well in a neighbour's garden.

There were two bedrooms upstairs and a really large bathroom, with a bath – but only cold water, flush toilet and an open fire grate. A trap door in the bathroom ceiling led into the roof space which housed the water tank, shared with next door. The bathroom fire was only lit to keep the water tank from freezing in winter.

Friday night was bath night. There was no hot water supply until much later when a Mr Richens, a rather large man I remember, installed a hot water tank high up in the kitchen. There was a tin bath in the kitchen. When father got back from the War he carried buckets of water from the copper outside up to the bathroom on Fridays. The same bathful of water had to do for each one of us in turn. Hair was washed in the scullery sink in soft rainwater from the pump, with 'green' soft soap. Amani was probably the first shampoo on the market – we talked of 'Amani night'.

All the bedrooms, except the attic, had open fireplaces. A fire lit in a bedroom usually meant someone was ill in bed. The stairs leading to the attic were never carpeted in my time. For many years I scrubbed those wooden stairs to earn my 6d a week pocket money. A skylight above was operated by a rope tied to the banisters. I remember the large double attic bed with its iron railings top and bottom and the brass knobs which unscrewed. And the quickest way down from the attic was via the banisters. From the attic window on a clear day one could see the clock on Ascot Racecourse. We had a second flush toilet, outside, but built in as part of the house. And in the garden the indispensable wash house with copper and coal shed.

As everyone had clean clothes for Sunday and all the beds had been changed, Monday was usually washday. So early Monday morning the copper was filled with buckets of water from the scullery sink, the fire was lit and more saucepans of water heated on the kitchen range. First there was a rough washing in the sink with Sunlight Soap. Very dirty items were scrubbed on a washboard. All sheets, table linen and underwear were of white cotton. These were boiled in the copper with hard white soap, shredded. Reckitts Blue Bag was added to the final cold water rinse to improve the whiteness.

Then there was the wringing, either by hand or in the mangle with its large wooden rollers. Mangling was not straightforward – buttons and fastenings had to be pushed to one side, at the same time turning the heavy handle and avoiding pinching one's fingers. Next outside, pegging all on a long clothes line stretching down the garden path. If the washing was less than pristine white the neighbours would notice! And to cheer up faded coloureds Drummer Dyes had a range of colours to choose from. Cottons were boiled up in the dye solution with a salt rinse to fix the colour. Table linen and the men's stiff detachable shirt collars of the day were starched with Robin Starch. It was important to catch the washing whilst it was still damp, so there was much running in and out to check. Items were rolled tight to distribute the dampness evenly throughout and left in a laundry basket for the next stage – the ironing. The heavy flat irons were heated on the top of the kitchen range. To test the heat of the iron you held the iron with an iron-holder slightly away from you face, or you spat on it – if it sizzled it was very hot! I still have our old flat irons – they make wonderful weights and door stops. Finally, the clothes had to be thoroughly aired – on the high rack in the kitchen or hanging over the fire guard round the open fire. No time for cooking on washday. Dinner, at midday was cold meat left over from Sunday's joint with mashed potatoes.

World War I

I have a vivid memory of us with my mother, Aunt Rose (Walter) and young Cousin John playing on a beach, possibly Broadstairs, when suddenly everything changed. Uncle Bert (Walter) came rushing down the beach saying we must go home at once as war was imminent. Uncle, being a commercial traveller, had a car. Meanwhile father had volunteered to join the Seaforth Highlanders. He enlisted on 16 September 1914 as No. 265672 Seaforth Highlanders attached to F. Company, 53rd (YS) Battalion Gordon Highlanders, Tillicoultry. Early training was in Scotland.

My father George Luther Peacock in uniform

In August 1915 father arrived at Blair Atholl after a 90-mile march from Elgin. So as to be near father as for long as possible, Mummy took Joan and me to Scotland. We travelled by train overnight, in a 'Ladies Only' carriage. Sleeping stretched out on a train seat was a new experience for us. Meantime, Fair View was let to Mrs Harold Biggs for 10 shillings a week.

I have odd memories of our stay in Scotland, a sitting room, with windows to the floor, jutting out over a rushing highland stream, with the Highlanders in their kilts marching through the heather, bagpipes playing. Mummy often talked of Blair Atholl, the Pass of Killicrankie, Pitlochry, Blairgowrie and Crieff.

Some battalions of the 51st Division were then drafted to France but others, including father's Company, remained along the east coast until 1917 as it was feared the Germans might invade. Bedford was the Headquarters of the 51st Division.

We three travelled down through East Anglia in the wake of the Battalion. This journey conjures up more names for me – Holt, Sheringham, Cromer and Kessingland. I can still picture the cliffs above Cromer, brilliant with scarlet poppies, and Norwich (father was there in May 1916). Here, as we slept three in a huge double bed, came an air raid warning.[3] I was hauled out of bed, very disgruntled, and pushed under the bed. At Kessingland there were still more poppies. At last back to Fair View. Brother Roy was expected in January 1917 and I had already missed a year's schooling.

Sometime during the war we had a visit from father's Commanding Officer Company Sergeant Major Catto. I can see him now, a red-headed Scot, passing the window very early in the morning. Breakfast was being cooked on the hobs in the dining room.

Seaforth Highlanders, Company Seargeant Major Catto (centre)
with father on the right

Back home, one day early in the War, there was a trip to London. Mummy, Joan and I met up with a Mrs Andrews, the wife of father's long-time friend. We were to visit a

[3] The first zeppelin raid was 19 January 1915, when three flew over Yarmouth, Cromer and Sheringham.

photographer – I think we must have been late for our appointment as I remember being hurriedly dragged by this strange lady's hand past the high fence surrounding the tennis courts at Wimbledon. I was unhappy and definitely cross!

Studio portrait London 1914

Another wartime memory, we two girls together in Mummy's bed on Sunday mornings scanning the casualty lists in the newspaper.

At Roy's birth on 23 January 1917 our family doctor, Dr Montgomery, attended and 'Nurse' came and stayed for a whole month whilst Mummy rested in bed, a common practice in those days. Nurse (I never knew her by any other name) did everything.

Then my first day at school which according to the Alwyn

Elsie Maud Peacock 1916

Road School registers was on 14 May 1917. I well remember standing outside the front gate, held firmly by the hand, with Mummy accosting the first 'big girl' who came along – this happened to be Joan Piercey from Top Common – asking her to: "Please take Mary into school".

Alwyn Road infant's class was on the sunny side of the building. I was very happy there. Possibly I had learned to read before starting school. I was fascinated by a picture on the blackboard in coloured chalks drawn by the teacher, Miss Round (or Pound). It illustrated the story of the Good Samaritan with Arabs in all their colourful robes. I wondered how could anyone be so clever with just coloured chalks!

Meanwhile Grandma Robson was arranging to leave her home in London to keep house for her bachelor son Robbie who was working in Manchester. They were to live in a tall, semi-detached Victorian house in Barlomoor Road, Didsbury.

Grandma, Mary Elizabeth Robson

Mummy was involved in this move from London. In October 1917 we three children and Mummy were in Manchester with Grandma. Alwyn Road School register gives my last attendance as 15 October 1917 – cause of leaving: 'London and Manchester'. I have only one indelible memory of that time in Didsbury – Roy, just walking, stood by the kitchen table, pulled on the tablecloth, tipping a boiling cup of Bovril down his bare front. We all screamed. For weeks the boy was wrapped in cotton wool. This must have delayed our return to Fair View because I did not get to school again until 9 April 1918 when Joan joined me at Alwyn Road.

The walk to school took Joan and me over the stile and across footpaths through Weall's fields to a bend with a boundary post and a large elm tree and then on through Headington's fields to Havelock Road, the edge of Maidenhead, almost a mile. As we always went home at midday we walked at least four miles every day. The footpaths were gravelled but it was much more fun to weave on the top of the bank through the stumps of the long-neglected hedges. There were no livestock only arable crops. I remember Dick Piercey and I sampling raw turnips on our way home one wintery afternoon – actually they tasted quite sweet. Our three brothers never experienced this exciting walk to school – by 1920 the footpaths had given way to Pinkneys Road.

Father spent some months in 1918 in Timperley Red Cross Hospital near Stockport on sick leave with a badly poisoned finger, cut whilst opening a tin. That finger was thereafter very stiff and disfigured.

Geoffrey was born at Fair View on 1 July 1918. It was a wonderfully sunny day. Joan and I, with Roy in the pram, were settled in the shade under the pear tree and told to stay there. Once again Nurse came to stay for a month.

Then on 11 November 1918 came the end of World War I. I had always averred that we had a half-day's holiday from school on Armistice Day – I remembered hurrying home across the fields. But then in 1989 Ray Knibbs in *Furze Platt Remembered* wrote that Alwyn Road School was closed for several weeks over Armistice due to the influenza epidemic then raging throughout the country. Peace celebrations were postponed until the early summer of 1919 and Alwyn Road had a tea party, possibly on a Saturday. So much for my memory – it was a sunny day I remembered, not a dismal November 11th.

Father was 'demobbed' on 20 February 1919 – official jargon "Disembodiment on Demobilization". The Audit Office, GWR at Paddington offered him his job back immediately on return to civil life.

For us two girls he brought home a small wind-up gramophone with one or two tiny records which we played endlessly, jigging around on those bare boards in the drawing-room. Over and over – "Way down in Tennessee" and "The roses round the door make me love mother more".

Donald (George Donald) was born at Fair View on 14 December 1920. By then the making of a new road into the Pinkneys Road housing development had reached Kent's Corner. Workmen outside Fair View laid straw to lessen the noise whilst the baby was being born. Over that Christmas Joan and I were packed off to Grandma in Didsbury so did not see our baby brother until January 1921. There was a memorable, so very exciting, journey up to Manchester, the two of us wrapped up in the dicky seat of Uncle Bert's GWK. It did not matter that it was winter time and dark.

This was a Christmas never to be forgotten. Grandma's Victorian house in Didsbury had commodious, high-ceilinged rooms, with open fires, the bathroom right up the top and cellars below. In the sooty back yard just outside the cellar door, there grew a clump of Himalayan balsam (or Policeman's Helmet) with explosive seed capsules. In the large drawing room with its chintz-covered chairs there was a long footstool, so, side by side, we could toast ourselves

Uncle Bert Walter with his GWK car

in front of the fire. And there was a piano, which was something of a novelty for us.

In a large corner house next door to Grandma lived a Mr and Mrs Knowles with their only daughter Margaret. Margaret, about my age, had striking auburn hair. We loved being next door to her. Being an only child, Margaret seemed to us to have everything. We spent hours in her wonderful Wendy house. We were invited to parties. One especially I remember – there was this large rocking horse, way up on a balcony, with children queuing up for a ride, but I was too shy to ask! (Many, many years later with some money left to me I bought just such a lovely rocking horse for visiting youngsters to enjoy).

Mummy made our party frocks – they were of sprigged muslin, lined for warmth, prettier than in this photo. To go with them she made brown velvet capes lined with pink satin. These were lovely. The sandals were of brown canvas. To produce those ringlets we had to suffer our hair wrapped in rags overnight by Grandma. White hair ribbons seemed to be the fashion.

And there was our first pantomime – "Where the Rainbow

*Christmas 1920 with Joan in party frocks
made by Mummy*

Ends" – it was breath-taking. The colour and the music – we sat transfixed. There in Manchester Joan and I gathered a bevy of new 'Aunts' – the Sirett 'girls' from Bramhall and Cheadle. There was Jean, who in 1925 married Uncle Robbie, with her four sisters – Tid, tall and handsome, Dorothy (Dolly) Whyte with small daughter Pam. Pam never knew her father – having gone through World War I he died in the 1918 'flu epidemic. I think Dolly was the better-off member of the family. I remember too that it was always impressed upon us that 'Whyte' was spelled with a 'y'. Then there was May, always elegantly dressed and Nell who was an invalid who later died, reminding me of Beth in *Little Women*. I was never sure where Auntie Kitty fitted in but she was so kind and produced such lovely meals! There was also a Sirett brother but I only heard tell of him.

Most of the Sirett family including Pam, Aunts Rose and Winnie with young Leslie, Grandma Robson and Mummy and Mr and Mrs Norris were all present at the wedding of Uncle Robbie and Jean Sirett in Manchester on 26 September 1925.

26 September 1925
Marriage of Uncle Robbie and Jean Sirett

I have no memories of the journey back home. Then there was this new babe – Joan and I were allowed to choose a name for him. So Donald it was, but with George first, after father. We were all gathered in the front bedroom round the fire – it was still January. Geoff aged 2½ was sitting beside me on the windowsill when suddenly he unlatched the window and fell out. It was frightening – we all rushed to the door, Mummy crying out "Is he dead? Is he dead?" as father carried Geoff, screaming his head off, up the stairs. As it happened he was quite unharmed. He had fallen on soft soil, narrowly missing the tiles along the edge of the flower bed. Geoff remembers it well – he was very annoyed that he was not allowed to walk up the stairs by himself. Dr Montgomery advised that he should rest for a day or two!

Mummy's business card

After Grandfather Robson's death Grandma, with the help of her daughters, moved back to London and set up a dressmaking business at her home, 20 Markham Square, Chelsea. The millinery side of the enterprise was Mummy's concern. She made beautiful hats for the ladies of Chelsea and Pimlico.

Mummy made all our clothes, even the boys' shirts and (short) trousers, stitching them on her Frister & Rossman sewing machine.

The youngest Robson daughter, Winifred, our Aunt Winnie, very soon married one of the Norris boys, Edgar, an engineer with GEC. She often told us the story of her 6-week long journey on a cargo boat to join Uncle in Shanghai. She could not possibly wait for the scheduled passenger service. Periodically over many years there came parcels with bales of silk from Aunt Winnie in Shanghai and later Hong Kong. We were all dressed in silk.

The Garden at Fair View

Across the bottom of the two gardens, Fair View and Ashton Cottage, there was, in the very early days, a strip of land belonging to a Mrs Cannon of Walnut Tree Cottage. She had quite a smallholding – her chicken, geese and ducks grazed outside on the Common. Later she let us have that strip of land so that our gardens were extended right to the wooded ground of Clarefield's boundary. As Fair View was built on what were the gardens, running South, of four or five cottages known as Walnut Tree Cottages, demolished in 1895, our garden had a legacy from those long-ago gardeners in the shape of two mature fruit trees, a pear and a greengage. Both were in full bearing – the pear was a Williams with a cooking variety grafted on. We always had tremendous crops. I remember the attic floor covered in ripening pears. Those fruit trees must have been planted by very skilled gardeners in the 19th century.

Father immediately set about cultivating the plot. I can see him now, arriving home from the station on his bike, then a quick meal and, in the dark evenings, digging by the light of a hurricane lamp. We soon became self-sufficient in vegetables.

Mummy, although London born, took to gardening like a duck to water. She bought all her seeds from Unwins – wallflowers, sweet williams, antirrhinums, nemesia, especially the newly introduced blue nemesia, and wonderful sweetpeas. As she became more adventurous she tried more half-hardy species such as cannas. She was an avid reader and she was delighted when Uncle Arthur's *Encyclopaedia of Gardening* (18th edition by T W Sanders, price 7s.6d.) came to her. It became her bible. I still treasure this book, now rebound by me. Dress boxes carefully packed with flowers and sacks of potatoes were regularly sent by rail to Grandma in Manchester. There were always flowers around the house. There is a story in the family of young brother Roy at Alwyn Road School who in a composition on 'Your tea table' wrote: "We always had flowers on the table even though the cups and saucers were odd".

Father inspecting Mummy's flower borders

Then in 1920, at the very outset of the housing development along Pinkneys Road, father immediately bought the first plot adjoining Fair View to ensure that no house was built alongside. So we had half an acre more garden.

Over the years we grew more vegetables and fruit, we kept chicken, White Wyandottes I remember, and for a while pretty little bantams, good layers of their tiny eggs. The flower garden developed enthusiastically by Mummy and the front lawn which started off as just farmland, allowed to green over and then constantly mown, was just large enough for some sort of cricket and rounders (any broken windows being paid for out of pocket money).

There were many family parties in the garden.

Mummy by her roses in Fair View garden

28

Playing cricket in the garden

Mother, Aunt Rose, Grandma Robson, Geoff and Donald (in front)

We had a small tent in the corner for sleeping outside in the summer, but after a few years it became too noisy from the traffic on the road outside.

In the garden on my 21st birthday with Cousin John

Our tent on the front lawn

As we reached our teens it was decided that we needed a tennis court! So the bottom half of the plot was laboriously dug over, loads of special turf ordered and I do so remember Mummy spending hours on end laying turves one at a time, checking with a spirit level as she moved along. Then with a second-hand tennis net, a line marker and the whole surrounded by high netting we were into tennis. Over the years until the outbreak of war in 1939 Mummy's tennis court was enjoyed by so many. I seemed to spend a lot of time re-marking lines in preparation for the next session – I wasn't much good at tennis.

Cousin Leslie Norris who was lost in the Merchant Navy in 1940, with Donald

Tennis parties at Fair View

Daily Life in the Fair View Neighbourhood

From Mummy's chance remarks of her battles with a kitchen range it seemed that not every meal turned out as expected. She had little experience of cooking and had only *Mrs Beeton's Household Management* to guide her. Her mother (our Grandma Robson) was a good cook – she had been a cook-housekeeper in her younger days. All through those early years at Fair View, with no gas or electricity but only the kitchen range and the open dining room fire for cooking, Mummy produced good regular meals with what was available.

There has come down to me a very tattered notebook of family recipes written in many different hands. Among the first, from Aunt Jean in Manchester around 1920, is one for bread, using lard, others for Wallop cake (with lard and Quaker oats), Parkin and 'German' cake. 'German' cake, being economical and filling, was one of Mummy's favourites. For the duration of World War II the name was changed to 'Dutch' cake. From Grandma Robson's pen we have apricot jam and gooseberry chutney, Mummy's contributions are bottling fruit the cottage way, a steamed pudding with fat (with dried egg) and a 'cheat' Christmas pudding. Then lemon pie and scones from Auntie Rosie. And in our schoolgirl handwriting recipes from our cookery classes with Miss Bell, whose marmalade and Christmas pudding instructions have been followed for many years.

There were always many mouths to feed – with seven of us, four of the Walter family frequently visiting and Grandma Robson we were often twelve or more. Father was a stickler for punctuality so meals were at regular times. Sunday's breakfast was always promptly at 9 o'clock whatever one was doing. Breakfasts were 'cooked' – porage, bacon and eggs, bread, butter and marmalade. We got through hundreds of pounds of home-made marmalade each year. Midday dinner had to be at 1 o'clock sharp to allow us all to get home from school and back again. This was the hot meal of every day except for washdays. The leftover Sunday roast provided several more meals – cold on washday, slices chopped small on a board to make a savoury mince on Tuesday, the rest with any bones and gravy with added stewing beef or neck of mutton and vegetables, made into a stew, slowly cooked in a large saucepan on the top of the stove.

At the end of the week, possibly Saturday there was a more extravagant meal – a thick, juicy rump steak, or fresh fish, herrings or plaice. Roast chicken seemed to be reserved for high days and holidays like Christmas and Easter, or for when there were visitors.

There was always 'pudding' – filling suet roly-poly, fruit pies and tarts, milk puddings – rice, ground rice, semolina, tapioca, blancmange, macaroni, and custard with stewed fruit. We children soon learned how to make custard in a hurry, even on a wayward Primus stove.

And then there was junket – warm milk, vanilla-flavoured, was set by adding rennet and topped with nutmeg. This made a very soft curd with a little whey. The schedules of local Agricultural Shows often included a class for junket-making! Rennet was used in cheese-making and so was readily available.

Tea was bread, butter and jam or fish paste, (salmon and shrimp, I remember), with home-made cakes and jam tarts, in that order – no cake until you had eaten your bread and butter. On Sundays there was thinly sliced Hovis brown bread with perhaps sardines or pilchards. In winter time a special treat in front of a glowing fire was hot toast oozing with dripping. There was always plenty of dripping from the roast joints – it was also used for frying. Father arrived home regularly at 6 o'clock each day – a portion of the mid-day meal had been saved for him. There was no supper as such but as we got older we could help ourselves to bread, butter and cheese laid out on the dining room table. Hot milk was also provided.

Shopping for most basic necessities was possible in the village. Mr Brown who owned an orchard over the Green sold fruit and vegetables and Mr Hunt of Middle Close (now Farthings) sold vegetables. Our main meal of the day was always based on 'meat and two veg'.

We had no butcher on the Green until much later when Mr Bartholomew set up his shop in Pinkneys Drive. So for fresh meat and fish we had to shop in Maidenhead.

Almost everyone in the village kept a few hens for egg production. In the daytime they ranged freely outside on the Green but were always shut in at night secure against foxes.

Eggs were only plentiful in the spring when hens by their very nature would lay a clutch of eggs and if left to their own devices would go broody and sit to hatch them. To keep the hens laying as long as possible eggs were continually removed. This was long before breeders had achieved an all-the-year-round egg-laying strain. So eggs were scarce in winter. They could be preserved in large crocks in an isinglass solution, but these were only suitable for cooking. There were very many breeds of poultry, some, the lighter Leghorn-type for egg-laying, the heavier ones for birds for the table. We kept chickens when we had more garden.

Bread, white crusty Cottage and Coburg loaves was delivered daily by our 'midnight' baker, Mr Deadman from Cookham Dean – it was usually late evening by the time he reached Fair View. Milk from Pinkneys Farm was ladled into milk can and jugs from a churn on Mr Debbidge's cart outside on the Green. Eventually, when Pinkneys Road became passable, milk was delivered from Maypole Dairies in Maidenhead in one pint and quart bottles. By then milk was by law pasteurized, and so would keep fresh much longer.

Practically everything else was available at John Roberts' village shop which also served as the Post Office. Very little was pre-packed – any amount could be weighed out from slabs of butter, whole cheeses, sides of bacon, all on the counter beside the bacon slicer. Sugar was loose – it was weighed out as required into screws of blue paper. It was always blue for sugar. Biscuits were weighed from large tins into paper bags. Broken biscuits were sold cheaply.

**Pinkneys Green Village Shop and Post Office
with 'free-range' poultry**

Ranged along the shelves were large jars of sweets – fruit gums, 'gob-stoppers', liquorice allsorts and twists of sherbet, but as mother considered sweets an unnecessary extravagance, we did not buy sweets! Joan and I were so thrilled when allowed to spend our pocket money with John and Bob at a sweet shop in Southfields. But one Christmas there came from Auntie Jean in Manchester a really tall tin of Fox's Glacier Mints, this being kept out of our reach in that high cupboard in the dining room. Those mints, doled out a few at a time, lasted a very long time. The empty tin with it's screw-top lid is completely air-tight and has been

The Fox's Glacier Mints tin

used as our biscuit tin ever since, painted in a different colour to match the kitchen décor as we moved house. I still use it today (2009).

John Roberts could supply almost anything in the household line, perhaps the most important being paraffin

John Roberts' shop

for oil lamps. He regularly called for the grocery order and delivered it on his bicycle. Besides running the very busy village shop John Roberts had been Pinkneys Green sub-postmaster for many years, first in a part of the house Gorseway, and later in a newly purpose-built house with the shop next door.

In earlier years the Post Office had been housed in one of the Town Hall Cottages near Kents Corner, moving into the village around 1900. The post came through Maidenhead. Delivery and dispatch included Sundays.

The post was our main means of communication. A penny (1d.) postcard arrived the next day and even on the same day. A stamp for a letter cost 1½d (three ha'pence). For more urgent messages there was an efficient telegram service. The written message was handed in and delivered at the other end by a telegraph boy on a bike. There were few private telephones – in an emergency Wally Piercey, landlord at the Waggon & Horses would allow us to use his. As it was not usual for ladies to go into pubs, it had to be father or one of the boys who phoned.

In the early days there were frequent trips to Maidenhead, on foot with Mummy pushing the pram with children on board or tagging along. Mummy had a key to open the farm gate for the pram. Maidenhead was good for hardware, china and shoes.

One such trip remains in my memory – Mummy with four of us, with pram, shopping in Maidenhead's High Street. As she went from shop to shop we stood guard outside with the pram. Finished at last, we set forth up Castle Hill towards home when Mummy suddenly realised that she was a child short. So back to the High Street to find Roy patiently waiting outside a shop, as he had been told to do. Panic over!

The Walter Family

In 1909 Mummy's younger sister Rose married Albert Edward Walter (Bert). They set up home in Southfields where their two sons, John and Bob, were born.

Uncle Bert and Aunt Rose Walter   *Cousins John and Bob Walter*

Uncle Bert was a commercial traveller, first with a German oil company until the outbreak of war in 1914. Then for the Avon Rubber Company dealing in motor tyres. Uncle's first car was a 2-seater GWK with a dicky seat, one of the models made by GWK Ltd of Maidenhead between 1914 and 1931. With a car, every opportunity was taken to exchange London's polluted, smoggy atmosphere for the fresh air of Pinkneys Green. So on a Sunday, perhaps once a month, they came in time for breakfast at Fair View. This enabled us children to have a long day together.

Uncle Bert's next car was a Horstman.

HORSTMANN (GB) *1914–1929*

Horstmann Cars Ltd, Bath, Somerset

The Horstmann started life as one of the more interesting and enterprising light cars. Its original engine was a 1-litre, 4-cylinder unit (enlarged in 1919 to 1½ litres), with a detachable head and horizontal overhead valves. The vertical rockers were operated positively by the camshaft. The valve gear was totally enclosed in a very tidy fashion. Forward of the flywheel, there were no chassis side members as such; the crank-case was extended to form the front of the frame and an undershield. The three forward speeds were housed in the back axle. The suspension too was unusual, consisting of cantilever springs and anti-roll bars at each corner. At the Junior Car Club's Burford Bridge rally in 1914, a Horstmann won the prize for the car with the most novel features: quite an achievement in an age when small-car design was extremely varied. By 1919 a full set of side curtains came with every car, a rare luxury in a light car of the time. A side-valve Coventry-Simplex engine of 1,386cc or 1,498cc was by this date available as an option, and by 1921 had supplanted the Horstmann engine altogether. Dashing sports and super sports models were offered, as well as the normal touring car, and all were now called Horstmans, with English rather than German spelling. By 1923, the basic model was the 12/30hp with a 1½-litre side-valve Anzani engine. In 1924 it was joined for a year by the 9/20hp, with a 1,100cc Coventry-Simplex unit. 1925 Horstmans were the first British light cars to have Lockheed hydraulic four-wheel brakes. They also had 4-speed gear-boxes. However, they were very expensive, and could not compete with the big manufacturers. Horstman tried, and failed, by cost-cutting: the 1928 range consisted of the Anzani-engined car with normal, mechanical brakes, and a 9/25hp with 1¼-litre engine and three forward speeds. They were now much cheaper. The company's interest in unusual systems of suspension persisted to the end. In 1929 they were experimenting with a system of independent suspension by coil springs, but this did not find its way on to production cars and in any case no more of these were seen after that year. TRN

*The **Horstman** parked outside **Fair View***

With transport we could go further afield for our picnics. Hurley, where we could swim in the river by the weir was a favourite place.

Picnics and swimming at Hurley Weir

41

John and Bob spent many a summer holiday with us, roaming the Thicket, joining in all our escapades. The family were nearly always at Fair View over Christmas – I often wonder where everyone slept. A single bed pulled from the wall, the ironing board on two chairs inserted and cushioned with eiderdowns made a double bed adequate for Joan and me.

We loved those Christmases with all the preparations – pudding-making days stoning raisins, washing currants and sultanas, chopping apples and dates and the final stirring. We made paper chains and decorated the tree with real candles. Santa always brought us stockings to be opened at the crack of dawn, filled with intriguing odds and ends and maybe an apple, an orange and a piece of coal (for luck), certainly nothing expensive. Uncle always came with a game in which we could all take part.

The highlight of the day was Christmas dinner at midday, a capon or turkey with all the trimmings, most important for father the bread sauce, vegetables and especially the Brussels sprouts, picked that morning from the garden by us children, sometimes our fingers numb with the cold.

There was cold chicken and ham with pickles for supper and afterwards we always played the traditional Christmas game 'Tibbits' round the dining room table.

By 1920 gramophones were much improved, but still wound up by hand. On the Sunday visits John brought his gramophone and collection of records of the current popular music – songs of Peter Dawson and Paul Robeson, Flotsam & Jetson, Ernest Clough's "Oh for the wings of a dove" – much to our delight. It was John who introduced us to Promenade concerts then in the Queens Hall where we queued up for a seat in 'The Gods'.

Outdoor Pursuits

From a very early age we children spent more time outside than in. As a little girl, gazing over the garden fence, I saw Mr Weall's hedger and ditcher, old Mr Friar, who had no nose but just two holes, clearing the ditch which ran along outside. Then there was Mr Weall's test of a new ploughing method – a steam roller on either side of the field and the plough, unattended, running suspended between the two. Greatest excitement of all, a small bi-plane standing in the field, the first aeroplane I had ever seen.

Outside on the Common there were always passers-by – the shortest route to Maidenhead was over the stile and across the footpath. One day a lady's handbag was left on the stile. Joan and I took it indoors. The very elegant lady who claimed it was so grateful that she presented us with a lovely edition ot *Black Beauty* which we read over and over again.

I remember the tramps who walked from Henley Workhouse to their next port-of-call, Maidenhead Union. After one day's casual work and two nights' stay they had to move on. So they walked from Henley to Stubbings, through the Thicket and over our stile at Kent's Corner. To my knowledge they never caused any trouble in the village. There was one old tramp who lived permanently on Pinkneys Green. In a very large chalk pit on the thicket opposite Wayside he had hewn out a very adequate shelter for himself from the solid white chalk.

Most villagers kept a pig. One day as I lingered outside the front gate two men came towards the stile pulling a hand cart with a large white pig atop, secured with a net.

I thought maybe they were on their way to Maidenhead, but no, not a bit of it – they promptly cut the pig's throat as I watched, wide-eyed. Then with a bundle of straw they lit a bonfire in the bushes and there and then burned the bristles from the carcass and returned from whence they came.

In the summer Mummy met us straight from school with a picnic – bread and butter and jam, cake (always home-made) and the old milk can filled with tea, all aboard the pram. Past Camley House towards the Bath Road there was a long grassy ride stretching as far as Thicket Corner – ideal for ball games.

Joan, Roy, Mary, Geoff and Donald 1922

On one such summer day in 1922 after our picnic, we were approached by a press photographer asking could we please pretend to be picking blackberries. We were only too willing to oblige.

A month or so later came my moment of fame – there I was, ostensibly picking blackberries, on the front page of the *Children's Newspaper* September 23rd, 1922. The *Children's Newspaper* (1919–1965) one of Arthur Mee's publications, was a weekly, price 2d. It grew out of the *Children's Encyclopaedia*, already on our bookshelf.

CHILDREN'S NEWSPAPER
September 23, 1922   Every Thursday, 2d.

Gathering the Blackberry Harvest—All over the countryside bushes heavy with ripe blackberries are being besieged by crowds of happy children, who carry the fruit home, where it is soon made into jam for the winter. No healthier fruit is found anywhere, and it is very prolific all over the British Isles

Enjoying the Commons

The Commons were gated to prevent grazing stock straying on to surrounding farmland. Until 1920 Randalls' cows, herded by Joe Randall, grazed the Commons throughout the summer, so keeping a very short sward over the chalk. In our time the stretch of the Common from behind the cricket pitch as far as Mr Brown's cottages and The Orchards was, until 1939, covered with gorse, criss-crossed with tracks made by the cows. Gorse had probably been grown there for centuries. The 18th century Lord of the Manor, Charles Ambler, allowed poor people to cut furze from Maidenhead Thicket for their own use. It had always been used for fuel and also provided foundations for corn ricks. In the village there are Furze Cottage, Furzeway and Gorseway and our local hamlet is called Furze Platt.

We all felt very protective towards our gorse-covered Common with it's flocks of linnets. One year we had an unusually dry Guy Fawkes' night and after our traditional village bonfire on the Green had died down some of the local lads decided to carry on by setting light to the gorse. A gang of us decided that this was not on so we spent the rest of the night beating out the flames after them. I only remember that we ended up very black.

Of the two long grassy rides, one stretched in a straight line from The Walnuts to Thicket Corner on the Bath Road. Records show that this was once used as a race course. The other ride leads from Wayside (earlier the Shoulder of Mutton) to Camley Corner on the Henley Road. It provided a short cut from the village to Stubbings Church and School. In contrast, along one side of Pinkneys Drive there were almost impenetrable thickets of hawthorn and blackthorn. I especially recall one summer day when, with John and Bob, we hacked our way on our hands and knees into the very centre of the solid mass of quickthorn and hawthorn. Inside we gradually cleared enough space to make a 'den'. The walls and floor we covered with bracken laboriously dragged in along the narrow tunnel. We spent many happy hours in our secret hiding place along with snacks and drinks from home.

Joan and I could not resist collecting armfuls of May blossoms. It was not allowed in the house – considered unlucky – so we decorated the walls of the large shed at the bottom of the garden. The scent was overpowering. We all picked wild flowers – violets, primroses, honeysuckle – the word 'conservation' had not entered our vocabulary. There was one notable exception, we had no bluebells to pick. But there were harebells and bedstraws on the grassy slopes of an old disused chalk pit over behind the cricket pitch. It was so sheltered, trapping the sun. Alas, now filled in as it had become a graveyard for old motor cars.

Over towards the Bath Road the grassy tracks were all 'up hill and down dale' – the result of flint-digging over the years. The unfilled pits and mounds of soil, all grassed over, made exciting rides on a bike.

In ancient times the whole area had been part of Windsor Forest. Over the centuries timber had been an important source of income for the landholders of the Commons and Thickets and the rights of the common people to remove wood for fuel had early been recognised. In our days the many trees on the Thicket, more especially those towards Stubbings House, were old, crowded and not managed in any way, a wonderful source of firewood for our open fires. On Saturday afternoons (father worked Saturday mornings – in fact everybody did) there were exciting 'wooding' expeditions – the whole family with the old pram for transport. Father was expert at bringing down dead branches – you just needed a heavy flint tied securely on

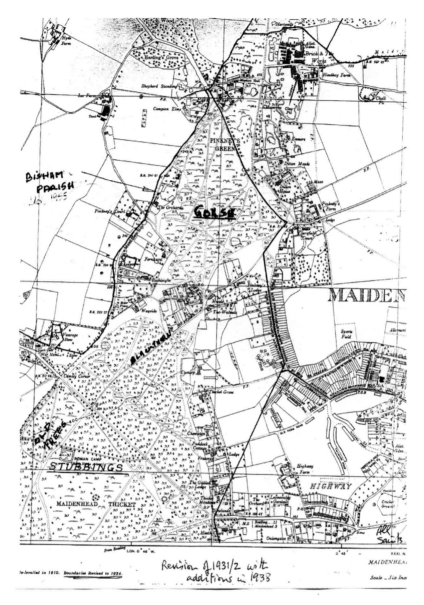

Ordnance Survey Map 1931/32 with 1938 additions

the end of a rope, flung over and pulled hard. We soon developed a good eye for a suitable log for the fires.

The 1875 Ordnance Survey map 2.5"/mile shows the wooded areas. Around the village itself the map indicates distinct rows of trees, mainly walnut, presumably planted by earlier Lords of the Manor – thus we have Walnut Tree Cottage and The Walnuts. These trees were fully mature in our time, bearing heavy crops of nuts. Squirrels permitting, every last nut was harvested by local lads up in the trees or bashing with sticks and stones from below. Some were picked green for pickling. The occupant of the first house built on the new Pinkneys Road development certainly did not endear himself to any of us when he had felled the last row of walnut trees on the Green, just because they impeded the flight of his homing pigeons.

The mature black poplars bounding the track outside Fair View (see page 7) were standing until 1920 when they were felled to make way for the Pinkneys Road development. Solitary oak trees marked property boundaries and elms the boundary curves. One such elm tree marked the half-way mark on our walk over the fields to school – to us it was just 'The Tree'. In fact it marked the boundary between the land of Pinkneys Farm and Highway Farm. Since 1934 the National Trust has planted and maintained trees around the village.

Birds abounded everywhere. We always maintained that nightingales kept us awake at night and there were so many cuckoos. Linnets in the gorse, yellowhammers in the hedges, goldfinches and dozens of house sparrows festooning our windows with their untidy nests. There were always larks overhead and flocks of pewits on the farmland surrounding the Common. Cereal crops were mainly autumn-sown allowing ground-nesting birds to rear their young undisturbed. But on the Common itself egg collecting was an accepted hobby and a few of the local lads occupied themselves bird-nesting or 'pugging' as it was called – just wanton destruction of any nest they came across.

Bird-catching for the cage-bird market (linnets and goldfinches) had been going on for hundreds of years. We remember at least one villager who was said to catch birds.

WH Hudson, a famous naturalist, stayed in the area on several occasions around 1900. He became acutely aware of the depredation of bird life on the Thicket and Common caused by the netting of birds for the song-bird trade. In this respect Cookham Rural District Council Minutes in September 1901 reported that application had been made for an Order to protect all birds on Sundays when the professional bird-catchers from towns were most active in the country. Later in 1913 the Wild Birds Protection Society moved that Maidenhead Thicket be made a protected area.

Brother Geoffrey enthusiastically studied our local bird population as he roamed the Thicket, his only guide book a set of cigarette cards. Over the years he became very knowledgeable. I was not quite so dedicated – my wanderings were always accompanied by a dog – but I so well remember the abundant red shrikes and the nightjars.

At that time there was a Mr Edgar Chance living at Bulwell on the Henley Road. He was a business man and ornithologist, who collected birds' eggs, especially those of the cuckoo for scientific study. The story goes that he paid the local lads pence for every cuckoo's egg they found. Geoffrey soon met up with Edgar Chance and was invited to see the egg collections housed in cabinets at Bulwell.

When he left Pinkneys Green Mr Chance continued his research at other sites. In October 1947 the Natural History Museum purchased his whole collection for £1,700 (personal communication, Natural History Museum, October 2002). It comprised five cabinets containing a 'general' collection of eggs, a mahogany cabinet with cuckoos' eggs and a small cabinet with eggs of the red shrike (over 20,000 eggs in total). All his data cards, notebooks, manuscripts, etc. were included. The results of Chance's work appeared in several publications. Another memory of Edgar Chance – he tried, unsuccessfully, to introduce the American Red Cardinal to the Thicket.

Childhood Friends – the Pryer and Hutt Families

Joan and I had known the two Pryer girls, Mavis and Joy, at school and the family's move to their new bungalow, Elm Nook, was the start of a life-long friendship. One of our very early activities together was prowling around the house-building sites along the new road. We found we could swing along the cross bars of the wooden scaffolding. I remember too our balancing acts along the top of a solitary 5-barred farm gate that is still standing.

We were out of doors whenever possible, roaming the Thicket studying the trees and wild flowers. Botany was in fact my favourite subject at school. We collected seeds, berries and nuts, planting them along the cinder drive at Elm Nook. Many years later they had formed an avenue of trees. In the dark evenings, gathered in their cosy sitting room, there was music. Mavis was the pianist – "In a monastery garden" her favourite.

A *boat trip* with Pryer family (also Pat Hoad and Tanis Henderson)

We were sometimes invited to join their Sunday trips to the coast. Mr Pryer's large open-top touring Armstrong Siddeley was loaded with rugs, towels and swim suits with a trunk full of Mrs Pryer's wonderful home-cooked meals strapped on the luggage rack and we were away, singing all the way, and waving to the soldiers through Aldershot.

Picnic on the way home from the sea

The most exciting trip of all – the annual Aldershot Military Tattoo held at Rushmoor – a wonderful searchlight spectacle with massed regimental bands filling the arena with their music. We joined in with the singing – "Abide with me" I especially remember. For us there was the added thrill of being out in the dark and not arriving home till around midnight.

There was a memorable visit to the British Empire Exhibition at Wembley in 1924. Along with piles of huge oranges from far-off places, we saw myriads of wasps sucked into the 'Wembley Rock' being made on site. All this and the helter-skelter too!

When the Pryer's' rough-haired terrier bitch produced a bunch of '57 variety' puppies, I begged father to let me have one of the dogs for myself. He agreed but with the proviso that I would be completely responsible for looking after him. This included paying the annual 7/6d. dog licence fee, mandatory at that time. And so Binkie (Binks) came into my life. He was quite unlike his mother – of more stocky build, smooth-haired, tan in colour with a few black hairs intermingled. He was definitely a one-man dog; after school hours he accompanied me everywhere. Dogs roamed free – motor traffic had not yet become a hazard. One time there was a short-lived rabies scare when all dogs had to be muzzled. Binks was always with me on visits to Roberts' shop. There was one memorable occasion when Mrs Brill, wife of the publican at the Stag & Hounds, was already in the shop together with her twin toddlers and her dog when Binks and I arrived. Immediately those two dogs flew at one another's throats. Mrs Brill, a rather buxom lady, clutching a babe under each arm, got herself up on to the bacon counter, legs a-dangling. I was left to deal with the dogs. One at a time I hauled them outside. Fortunately I was wearing gloves, so it must have been winter time.

By then the members of the family were following their own interests, and gradually one by one we acquired bikes so could get further afield – to schools in Maidenhead, Hurley for swimming, Cookham Dean for the cherry blossom. Cookham Dean for some reason was known as 'Kaffir Land' and I remember Roy talking of 'going up the treacle mines' to see his girl friend (the schoolgirl daughter of our Cookham Dean baker) I dismissed this strange label as just schoolboy jargon until very recently when, reading the Bootles *Story of Cookham* (1990) I came across the following:

"James Skinner, who grew up in Cookham Dean in the 1890's:
'In my young days there was always a Fair on (Dean) Common on Easter Monday, a great day! There were swings, cocoanut (sic.) shies, cheap jacks selling crockery etc. etc., buns on strings from the cross bar of the goal posts, dripping with treacle. Our hands were tied behind our backs and we had to eat them as best we could!'

We all spent many hours up at Lee Farm with the Hutt family. There were five children in the Hutt family, one girl and four boys and five of us with three boys. We got to know one another at primary school and eventually all the boys were in the Scouts together. For our three all that went on at the farm was fascinating – fetching in the cows, tractors, mowers, harvesters, rick building and so on.

Lee Farm was owned by a Mr Fisher, wealthy landowner and farmer – he also owned Court Farm at the bottom end of Lee Lane, then a poultry farm under a manager. Earlier this had been all one large Lee Farm. Mr Hutt was Manager, a very good farmer from a long line of farming folk. The farm was run on very up-to-date lines (for those days) with a fine pedigree herd of Dairy Shorthorns, with a huge prize-winning bull (called Babraham). There was a large fully equipped dairy next to the house and a dairymaid to deal with the milk and cream. Periodically there were open days and sales when a marquee was set up and caterers came in.

Cricket at Pinkneys Green

Pinkneys Green had a very flourishing Cricket Club. Any Saturday afternoon and sometimes on Sundays (but always finishing before Evensong) we could wander over the road to watch the game, sitting on the grass. Mr 'Johnnie' Walker of the Stag & Hounds was for many years President of the Club. In 1973 he wrote a short history of the Club with notes of some outstanding matches played over the years and photos of the players.

'Johnnie' Walker

Freddie Brown, England's Test player, often played cricket on the Green whenever he was staying at Fernhurst. Freddie first played for the MCC during their 1932/33 Australian tour, later becoming England's Captain and in 1971 MCC President. Roy was the cricketer in our family and there was one memorable occasion when he bowled out Freddie Brown.

Although the area was ploughed for food production in 1939 the future of the cricket ground was assured. After World War II the lime trees on the western boundary behind the cricket pavilion were planted in memory of Roy, who was lost in 1940.

Brother Roy in RAF uniform, he died in 1940

Local Schools

In our day there were two schools within reach of the village children – Stubbings Church of England School on the Henley Road, built by the then Lord of the Manor, Henry Skrine, founder of Stubbings Church. The school register dates from 1852. Until 1926 Stubbings was an Elementary School for boys and girls up to age 14, thereafter a Junior School for children to 11 only.

For many years Stubbings school room was the venue for parish functions – Sunday School, concerts, whist drives, Guide meetings, jumble sales, etc. It was finally closed in 1934.

Stubbings School 1921
Bob Prew who married my sister Joan is in the middle of the back row

Alwyn Road School, on the Maidenhead side, was opened in 1907 by Berkshire Education Committee and was planned to take 418 pupils aged from 5 to 14, with a spacious hall and eight classrooms. Pupils could try for scholarships or free places to the two local (fee-paying) secondary schools, Maidenhead County Boys and County Girls.

Alwyn Road School

The school doors at Alwyn Road were locked on the dot of 9 o'clock. So woe betide anyone late – you stood outside until your name was taken – punishment was to stay in after school.

We started every day assembled in the hall, the little ones in the front row. That first winter must have been very cold – hands painfully thawed out as we sang the old familiar hymns – "New every morning is the love", and "Now that the daylight fills the sky" and at the end of the school day "The day thou gavest Lord is ended" and "Now the day is over". We did have gloves – they were knitted, woollen, dangling on elastic threaded through our coat sleeves but did we ever wear them? In the early days everyone wore boots and the girls wore pinafores. I wore boots to school for a year or so – buttoned, needing a button hook.

In our time Mr Arthur Harris was Headmaster, a strict disciplinarian but well respected. He took our singing lessons. He was critical of our Berkshire accent with it's dropped T's and H's. He insisted on 'round English O's' with mouths open wide enough to take a match box on end. We constantly practised saying 'round the houses'. We sang from the New National Folk Song Book – "The harp that once through Tara's halls", "Drink to me only with thine eyes" and "Cherry ripe".

Classes were large, quite often 50 boys and girls together. We sat in desks in pairs facing the teacher and the blackboard. I seem to remember the boys rather than the girls – Walter Vaughan, Brian Lister, Dick Piercey – Dick lived at the Waggon & Horses two doors away from Fair View.

The daily curriculum was mainly the three R's – reading, writing and arithmetic. Reading books were handed out and one by one we read aloud. Laboriously we learned to write with pen and ink an almost copperplate script. An Ink Monitor filled the ink wells daily. We soon became adept at mental arithmetic as we endlessly chanted our 'tables' in unison.

We girls learned to knit, first, on large needles, we made children's reins in brilliant colours. Our knitting became quite professional – in my last term at Alwyn Road before secondary school each of us had made just one woollen sock, worked in the round on four steel needles, heels turned and toes grafted, so no seams. For the annual Sale of Work I remember having the job of pairing up those single socks, everyone knitted at a different tension. All the ends needed to be darned in neatly. Needlework was by hand, no sewing machines at school. We were taught hemming, tacking, over-sewing, blanket stitch, seams, double and run-and-fell. Early on we practised darning, a very necessary skill with all the woollen socks and stockings worn in those days.

I enjoyed our art classes with water colour painting of mainly flowers. We always took flowers to school. They stood in jam jars all along the window sills.

I can scarcely put names or faces to any of the teachers at Alwyn Road during my time there. There was one, a Mr Vivash, who must have made an impression and at sometime in about Class 4 there came a young man, maybe on teaching experience, who stirred our interest in geology and archaeology – on Saturdays he took us on trips to local gravel pits searching for fossils. Fascinating, but at the end of term he left. Disappointment all round.

There were no organised games at Alwyn Road School, but I think the boys played football. But according to the current craze we took to school, say, hoops one term, marbles the next, then tops and there was hopscotch and skipping and 'conkers'. Great competition. We collected sets of cigarette cards on all sorts of subjects, so our men folk were encouraged by the manufacturers to keep smoking. Father did just that practically all his life.

So, on reaching the age of 5, one by one the three boys followed Joan and me to Alwyn Road.

Joan's best friend at Alwyn Road was Rose Abercrombie. On Fridays after school we two went back to tea at her home in Courthouse Lane. Mr Abercrombie was a coal merchant and in the early days had two lovely heavy horses and a coal cart housed in sheds at the end of the garden with access to Alwyn Road. Whilst Rosie shared her toys with Joan, I got my head down and read all her interesting magazines and the *Children's Newspaper*, all new to me. Mrs Abercrombie's teas were scrumptious. After dark father came to collect us – he rode his bike across the fields with a hurricane lamp hanging on the handlebars and walked us home. In due course Rosie joined in all our escapades – climbing trees, fishing for tiddlers in Distins pond, walking, dancing, eventually becoming a member of the family when she married Cousin John.

In 1922, with a scholarship, I moved to Maidenhead County Girls. With more holidays than the rest of the family I went up to Grandma's on my own. Father put me on the train at King's Cross in the charge of the guard, to be collected by Grandma in Manchester. There I was thoroughly spoilt – visits to Belle Vue and the Zoo, rides on the helter-skelter wearing my new school hat. Asked what I would like for a special treat I plumped for tripe and onions and jam puffs.

Community Life in the Parish

Life in a village has always revolved around a church. But Pinkneys Green did not have it's own church until 1850. For hundreds of years before that the village had been part of the Parish of Holy Trinity Church, Cookham. It was some miles away, but where the villagers worshipped, registered their births, celebrated their marriages and buried their dead.

In 1825 Henry Skrine, the then Lord of the Manor of Cookham, bought Stubbings House. The Skrines were of an ancient family recorded from the mid-16th century in the parish of Warleigh near Bath. Henry purchased land from Mr G H Vansittart of Bisham Abbey and in 1849 proceeded to build Stubbings Church, the Vicarage, Stubbings Church of England School and Camley Cottages where Mr Penny and the Misses Penny lived for many years. The Church, St James the Less, was consecrated in 1850.

Stubbings Church built in 1849, consecrated in 1850

In 1929 the people of Pinkneys Green became concerned when the Trustees of the Pinkneys Green Library and Reading Room proposed to sell a former chapel built in 1860 in the grounds of Ditton House (see Peacock, 2009) and to give the proceeds to the fund for the planned Furze Platt Memorial Hall. Mr Emil Garcke of Ditton House wished to incorporate the building into his own property. So the villagers formed a Committee, to keep the building for the use of the community. First instigated by a Miss Brown of Hartwells on the Winter Hill Road. Father, among others, took an active part in the proceedings.

The proposal to sell was dropped and Mr Garcke generously offered to enlarge the hall and to build a separate reading room for the use of the village. The Pinkneys Green Club and Institute was officially opened in 1932. The Garke family took a keen interest in all it's activities. Emil Garcke encouraged us to join the British Empire Naturalists Association or BENA, and a few of us went on BENA's so-called 'Nature Walks'.

Mrs Garcke senior, a very elegant elderly lady, a member

On a BENA 'Nature Walk'

63

of the Dickens Society, set villagers the task of writing an end to the unfinished *Edwin Drood*. Father won the prize – a copy of Emil Garcke's *Individual Understanding. A Layman's Approach to Practical Philosophy* published in 1929.

The hall became the centre of the village. There were whist drives, ballroom dancing with dances once a month. A jolly, rotund Mrs Curtis from Maidenhead enthusiastically introduced us to old-time dances including the Gay Gordans, the Valeta and the Lancers, a very complicated set dance with dozens of different manoeuvres to be remembered.

Also concerned about the spiritual welfare of the villagers in the Golden Ball area who mainly worked in the brickfields were the Trustees of the Marlow Baptists, who as early as 1905 applied for permission to build a Mission Hall at Pinkneys Green. This building was much used in our days and was known to us as 'the Tin Tabernacle'. In 1922 and again in 1933 the Trustees applied for extensions. The Mission Hall has now long been demolished.

Our Vicar the Reverend W Outram came to the village in 1919. He was a gentle, learned man who regularly visited his parishioners. When Mr Outram knocked on the door

The Stubbings Vicarage

Mummy removed her apron, wiped all our noses and ushered us into the drawing-room for a short prayer.

We went to Sunday School at Stubbings. I, as a very little girl, always strayed off the beaten track over the Thicket, picking flowers on the way to the Vicarage, where we sat dangling our legs on a chintz-covered window seat in the drawing-room overlooking the garden. Miss Outram, the Vicar's daughter, taught us – she played the piano. "All things bright and beautiful" always takes me back to those lovely carefree days.

Sunday School for older children was over the road in the Schoolroom. Every week we learned the collect for the coming Sunday and for attendance there were colourful religious pictures on stamps for sticking in a book.

Two important parish functions were the annual jumble sale and the Church fete in the Vicarage grounds. In all parish affairs Mr Outram had the able assistance of Miss Hidden who was churchwarden, secretary to the Parochial Church Council and organist. She lived at The Cottage and if we ever had a problem we always went first to Miss Hidden.

The jumble sale was a great event – the whole village joined in the scramble for a good buy. Back from school we were always agog to see what mother had bought.

The Church fete catered for everyone. There were all kinds of races for the children (and grown-ups) – including three-legged, egg-and-spoon and tug-of-war. There was music, stalls of goodies, tea and cakes. Was it always as sunny as we remember it?

In 1927 the Rev Outram moved to a parish in Dorset and Dr Nairn came to Stubbings with his wife and a daughter who bred dogs. Dr Nairn had been Headmaster of Merchant Taylors School in London. He had a very loud voice and rode a bike around his parish. He officiated at the wedding of sister Joan and Bob Prew on 22 August 1939.

Guides and Scouts in Pinkneys Green

Around 1925 Joan and I, with Mavis and Joy Pryer joined the Guides – the 1st Pinkneys Green (Miss Baden-Powell's Own), the first company in the world to be registered at the new Headquarters. Robert Baden-Powell had already tried out his scouting ideas at a Brownsea Island camp in 1907 and in 1908 published his *Scouting for Boys*. Then at the first Scout rally at Crystal Palace girl scouts asked for recognition. So in 1910 when Agnes, sister of Robert Baden-Powell, whilst staying with a friend, Miss Del Riego at White Cottage, Golden Ball Lane, Pinkneys Green, was besieged by the local girls, the 1st Pinkneys Green (Miss Baden-Powell's Own) was born. We met in the old Stubbings Schoolroom

This 1924 photo shows our uniform – worn throughout our Guiding years
I am second on the right, front row

66

1st *Pinkneys Green (Miss Baden-Powell's Own)*

Marian MacDonald · Mary Peacock · Jane Randall · Mavis Pryer · Miss Arbouin · Nellie Allin (Co. Leader)

Amy Judd · Joan Hutt · Alison MacDonald

on Saturday afternoons. Captain was Miss Bateman, Lieutenants Miss Arbouin and Miss Outram, daughter of the Rev Outram at Stubbings. There were the three Macdonalds from The Orchards (Janet, Marion and Alison), Ann Fraser from Fratons, Joan Hutt from Lee Farm, Jane Randall, Cathy and Daphne Cullum and the Overs from Burchetts Green plus our Company Leader Nellie Allin – who cared for her mother who was confined to a wheel-chair. Other names elude me.

Meetings were somewhat regimented. We marched in the playground, forming fours with precision, raising our flag with ceremony. There was first aid, tracking and signalling with flags – military again. We learned our knots – reef, bowline, clove hitch, sheepshank, sheetbend and lashing. We played netball, and, indoors, a game known as 'duster

Mavis Pryer	Marian MacDonald	Mary Peacock	Joyce Pryer	Jane Randall	Joan Peacock	Janet MacDonald

Boat outing at camp

hockey' – two teams, a goal at each end, a duster and two sticks. We enjoyed country dancing. There was an old piano in the Schoolroom. We sang a lot – some of B-P's African tribal songs and "Jerusalem". Our first experience of camping was at Cowes on the Isle of Wight with other Maidenhead companies. We slept in Bell tents on groundsheets and straw-filled palliasses. Jobs were allotted – wood supply for the fire, cooking in large dixies and small billy cans, scrubbing 'lats' –wooden seats suspended over a deep trench, dug beforehand by the farmer. We swam in the sea – time in the water strictly limited and never less than an hour after a meal. There was a delightful rest hour after the midday meal when we lounged on our palliasses in the sun and the tuck shop was open

Total cost for 14 days holiday for each of us – 30 shillings!.

By now Pinkneys Green Scouts had a permanent home as the trusteeship of the Hall was finally taken over by the local Scout organisation.

Pinkney's Green Scout Hut, formerly the Library and Reading Room, built as a Chapel in 1860

Pinkneys Green Scout Troop continued to flourish in their new Headquarters, especially after the arrival of their new Scouter, Mrs Isobel Mitchell who had been running Scout troops in Scotland and came down to be near her sister Betty (Mrs Kenneth Garcke). All my brothers were Scouts.

My sister Joan together with Betty Garcke and later with Hilda Hutt, ran the Pinkneys Green Wolf Cub Pack in the 1930s.

There is a well-researched detailed history of Pinkneys Green Scouts by Don Astley (unpublished, 2000).

Scouting in the 1930s

Isobel Mitchell

Jack Brill
Roy   Bill Hutt
Donald

Roy   Bob Prew   Geoff
Donald

Betty Garcke and Joan 1931   *Some of the Wolf Cub Pack 1931*

Wolf Cubs in 1937

The Brickfields and other Developments

The geology of the upper part of Pinkneys Green towards Bigfrith and Cookham Dean, known locally as 'Top Common', produced rich deposits of brickearth.

In 1820 Charles Cooper and his son John Kingdom Cooper established the Pinkneys Green Brick & Tile Works. After a fire in 1906 only tiles were made at Pinkneys Green. Sometime in the 1980's the brickfields were closed down, and the business was re-named Maidenhead Brick & Tile Co. Ltd. The site together with it's engine sheds etc. are now owned by the National Trust.

With the need for new housing after the war, Cookham Rural District Council (RDC) Housing Committee was asked to open negotiations with owners of sites for 12 cottages opposite Pinkneys Farm. By September 1920 these discussions had proved unsuccessful. What happened next affected us all at Pinkneys Green.

Mr Weall of Pinkneys Farm, on obtaining the freehold of the property in 1920, promptly set about selling off as building plots his farmland along the footpath route from Kent's Corner towards Maidenhead, linking up with Miss Headington of Highways Farm who did likewise with her land from St Marks Road upwards towards Pinkneys Green. Mr Weall, a 'gentleman' farmer, had been a member of Cookham RDC since it's inception in 1895 and also of that Council's Planning Committee from 1900 until his death in 1927. There were no overall plans for his development, the plots were sold off one by one, buyers applying individually for planning permission for a house, bungalow, or whatever. Father at once bought the first plot adjoining Fair View so ensuring that no house was built close alongside and at the same time enlarging our garden by half an acre (see page 28).

The first building plans approved by the Planning Committee date from September 1920 – the first for WAJ Deeley (wooden bungalow), then for W Stubbles (wooden cottage) [When built this house was asbestos-clad] and on 1 November 1920 for Mr F Pryer (wooden bungalow) – this latter built well back from the footpath line almost to the boundary of The Walnuts.

Gradually over the next 10 years or more the building slowly went on, with single houses, cottages and bungalows of all different styles. In time local building firms began to buy up several plots together. At the same time house owners on Pinkneys Green itself were putting in plans for extensions to their properties. With the prospect of easier access to Maidenhead and the increase in the number of cars, more garages were needed.

Although we continued to feel protective towards our Common and Thicket, we soon came to realize that the link-up with Maidenhead considerably widened our horizons. We had been biking across footpaths to school but now we had a road to ride on. Back in 1921 there had been a Thames Valley bus service through Pinkneys Green. This linked Maidenhead via Furze Platt, Pinkneys Green and Stubbings with Bisham and Marlow. It also ran on Sundays. But now we had a direct bus service to Maidenhead from the Waggon & Horses, weekdays and Sundays, and late into the evening. We could get to the cinema – 'the pictures' – and I well remember Saturday evening 'four-penny pop concerts', once a month in the old Town Hall, provided by a different organisation each time. Early arrivals could get the best seats – all very uncomfortable. We walked there and back.

As families moved into the new houses we gained new friends, not only we children but the grown-ups too.

We soon got to know Mr and Mrs Deeley. Mr Deeley was in charge of the local cesspool emptier, a great black tanker.

The Deeleys had two grown-up children who came home occasionally – Dennis resplendent in aMerchant Navy, uniform and Nora, a lovely brunette. There was a memorable occasion for Joan and me – we were invited by the Deeleys to hear that wonderful new invention, 'the wireless'. The two of us were sat on a long low stool very close together so that we could share one headphone between us. And lo and behold, unbelievably there was music, very faint.

Schoolboys everywhere were talking of crystal sets and cat's-whiskers. Our first radio was an early Marconi. A tall pole, almost a telegraph pole, carried the aerial through an upper window. One day during a school holiday, Roy, Geoff, Donald and Cousin Leslie needed an aerial to try out a crystal set they had made, so down came the pole to be reinstated later. I well remember that father was not too well pleased when he got home from London.

The radio for us was a constant delight. Just one programme from Alexandra Palace – "2LO Calling". From those early days right through the 1930's we had many wonderful music hall programmes – Gracie Fields, the Crazy Gang, Elsie and Doris Waters, Clapham and Dwyer, Flanagan and Allen, Stainless Stephen, Gillie Potter, Mabel Constanduros and lots more. Ballroom dancing had become very popular. At 5 o'clock every day after school, Jack Payne and his band played dance music. Joan and I danced on the lino in the dining room. Henry Hall and his orchestra were Manchester-based and were friends of the Sirett sisters. And later came Victor Sylvester with his orchestra. Children's Hour I remember with Uncle Mac saying "Hello children, everywhere".

When Mr Weall died on 2 March 1927 Cookham RDC decided to take over the liability for maintenance and repair of the continuation of St Marks Road from Mr Weall's executors and from the owners of Highway Farm.

The RDC continued to oppose Maidenhead Town Council's

boundary changes in spite of Maidenhead's assurance that they would at once obtain powers for the proper maintenance of the Thicket and that all existing rights and liberties of the inhabitants would be carefully preserved.

Then in March 1929 the then Lord of the Manor, Miss ADM Skrine, sold the manorial rights to Odney Estates Ltd. This prompted a public meeting at Stubbings of local people anxious for the permanent preservation of the rural character of the Commons in the face of urban expansion around Maidenhead. A local committee raised a fund for the purchase of the manorial rights. The money was handed over to the National Trust for the management of the property as open space held for the enjoyment and benefit of the public.

By April 1932 Berks County Council (CC) stated that as there seemed no likelihood of an agreement being reached between Cookham RDC and Maidenhead Town Council, they would proceed to put forward their proposed scheme for the extension of the Borough. The boundaries were finally fixed. Thus it was that in May 1934 the Town Clerk of Maidenhead invited the officials of Cookham RDC to accompany the Corporation on the occasion of the perambulating of the boundaries of the new Borough.

In 1939 some acres of the open Commons (shaded on the map) were ploughed for food production. The areas were completely flattened, trees uprooted and buried in the old quarries and chalk pits. A poignant memory – with tears in our eyes a small group of us villagers stood silently outside Roberts' shop watching a great tree crashing to the ground. [The areas were derequisitioned in 1962 but continued to be cut for hay. The Commoners retained their grazing rights but the grassland had lost it's biodiversity].

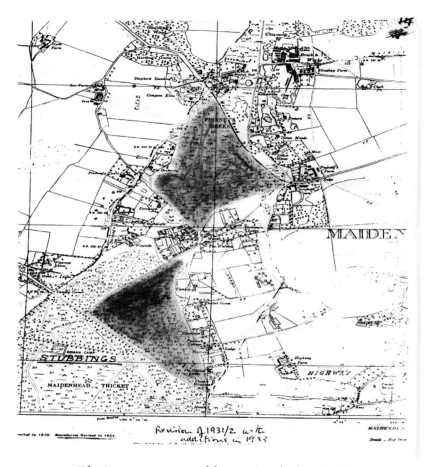

The Common areas used for wartime food production

Last Words

Around 1936 father bought a car – a Rover Ten coupé about five years old – for which he paid £40. From the book A–Z *of Cars of the* 1930's the car appears to have been one of the 1931 Weymann Coupés.

Father with his 1931 Weymann Coupé Rover 10

All six of us learned to drive in that little car – and we all passed the test first time! We had an excellent tutor in Mr Millar, chauffeur at Pinkneys Lodge. Every morning for about a fortnight I had a concentrated driving lesson before going to work. One very vivid memory – time and time again I practised parking 'Oggy' (OG was the registration number) between two huge brewers' delivery lorries off the Bath Road at Knowl Hill. We had to go to Slough to experience traffic lights as Maidenhead had none in 1937. We took the driving test in Reading. I (and my sister too) remembered driving up the hill past Reading Gaol (with shades of Oscar Wilde) Maybe it was especially difficult just there.

Joan's wedding to Bob Prew in 1939

Father rarely used the car himself but we were allowed to 'borrow' it if we recorded our mileage in a book kept in the car for this purpose. We paid father 1d a mile. The arguments that followed over the mileages unaccounted for were endless! Father paid for the petrol – the best was Shell at 1s.10d a gallon. With petrol rationing at the outbreak of war, use of a car at home was very limited so Donald, then in the RAF, took Oggy along with him. Our much-loved family car was eventually bombed on a bomber station "somewhere in England".

Meanwhile some of us had finished with school. For me, after matric at Maidenhead County Girls, a Dairy Science certificate course at Reading University, a brief spell milking cows, making butter and cheese, then a life-time job in the Information Section and as Librarian at ICI's Agricultural Research Station at Jealott's Hill. Joan had joined the office staff at the Widney Manufacturing Company in Maidenhead where she made a life-long friend in Madge Chinn. Joan and Bob (Prew) married in 1939. Roy, after leaving Maidenhead County Boys joined the Library Association and was on the staff of Maidenhead Public Library, learning to fly with the RAF Voluntary Reserve at White Waltham in his spare time. He was lost in 1940. Both Geoff and Donald, after County Boys, enrolled at RAF Engineering College at Halton.

So thus it was that on the outbreak of war in 1939 all three boys were immediately called up by the Ministry of Defence. The occasion of Joan and Bob's wedding on 22 August 1939 was the very last time the whole family was ever together.

Home on leave from the RAF, in May 1944 my brother Geoffrey (he who, as a small boy, survived falling from the bedroom window) married Elsie née Stevenson. To accommodate his growing family Geoff bought Fair View from father. In 1945 I moved with my parents to Henley-on-Thames, and continued working at Jealott's Hill until I retired from ICI in 1966 by which time I had become a member of the Chartered Institute of Library and Information Professionals. After father died in 1968 I took care of Mummy until her death in 1975. I then moved to a cottage in the garden of Watts Barn near Bristol where my brother Donald lived, before finally settling in my present home in Burbage in Wiltshire very close to my sister Joan and her husband Bob. I devoted my time in retirement to world travel, family history research, gardening, birdwatching and botanical watercolour painting.

Meanwhile, back at Fair View, Geoff's children were born: John in 1945, Margaret in 1947, Anthony in 1948 and Anne in 1953. Sadly Elsie died in 1958, leaving Geoff to manage this large household single-handed until he met and married Betty in 1968. Their son, David was born in 1969. The family eventually moved to Pewsey in Wiltshire in 1989 when Fair View was sold, thus severing its long association with the 'Peacock' family.

Fair View in the 21st century

FAIRVIEW, 106 PINKNEYS ROAD, MAIDENHEAD, BERKSHIRE, SL6 5DN

With views over National Trust Commons at Pinkneys Green to the front, a substantial older semi-detached house believe to have been built in the early part of the 20th Century. Offering excellent accommodation of character on three floors. There is parking to the front and good size gardens to the rear. Located in a prime residential area at Pinkneys Green. There are local shops and schools in the immediate vicinity with larger shopping amenities and railway station in Maidenhead Town Centre. The motorway network can be joined at Junction 8/9 of the M4. Features include character accommodation with large kitchen/breakfast room, four bedrooms two with en-suite shower rooms and family bathroom. Rarely available. Recommended for inspection.

RECEPTION HALL/STUDY: DINING ROOM: LIVING ROOM: SPACIOUS KITCHEN/BREAKFAST ROOM: UTILITY ROOM: CONSERVATORY: FIRST FLOOR LANDING: THREE BEDROOMS: TWO EN-SUITE SHOWER ROOMS: FAMILY BATHROOM: SECOND FLOOR LANDING: 30' FOURTH BEDROOM WITH DRESSING AREA (SPACE FOR EN-SUITE): PARKING SPACE TO THE FRONT: DELIGHTFUL REAR GARDENS WITH SPACE FOR FURTHER EXTENSION, SUBJECT TO PLANNING PERMISSION: PRIME LOCATION AT PINKNEYS GREEN: RECOMMENDED

Directions From Maidenhead Town Centre take the A4 towards Reading turning right at the mini-roundabout at the top of Castle Hill into St Marks Road. Follow St Marks Road into St Marks Crescent and Pinkneys Road where the property will be found on the right hand side just before the Green.

PRICE.........£395,000.........FREEHOLD

Bibliography

Ambler, Charles. 1790. *Reports of cases argued and determined in the High Court of Chancery, with some few in other courts*: London, printed by A. Strahan and W. Woodfall for T. Wheldeon. Court of Chancery Conference.

Ashmole, Elias. 1736. *The history and antiquities of Berkshire. With a large appendix of many valuable original papers, pedigrees of the most considerable families in the said County, and a particular account of the castle, college and town of Windsor*: by Elias Ashmole, Esq.; to which will be added the life of the author.

Ashmole, Elias. 1666. *A true copy of remarkable Epitaphs, and some very ancient Inscriptions, in all Churches, and other places, in the County of Berks. Taken in the year of the Incarnation 1666*: by Elias Ashmole Esq., Windsor Herald-at-Arms, and Deputy Marshal. From Sir Edward Bysshe, Knight, King at Arms, Clerencieux, for the County aforesaid. [Copy in Bodleian Library, Oxford].

Astley, Don. 2000. *History of the Pinkneys Green Scout Troop. A personal view by Don Astley*. Peterborough, Don Astley [unpublished].

Aston, M. E. 1967. *Thomas Arundel. A Study of Church Life in the Reign of Richard* II. Oxford, Clarendon Press.

Barber, Norman. 1994. A *Century of British Brewers* 1890–1990. New Ash Green, Kent, Brewing History Society.

Bootle, Robin and Valerie. 1990. *The Story of Cookham*. [Privately printed]. ISBN 9516276-0-0.

Burke, J. B. 1979 edn. *The Roll of Battle Abbey, annotated*. Baltimore Publ. Co. Inc. (Originally published London, 1848).

Chance, Edgar P. 1922. *The Cuckoo's Secret*. London, Sidgwick & Jackson.

Chance. Edgar P. 1937. *Some observations on egg collecting and other matters*. Burchetts Green, Berks, E. Chance.

Chance, Edgar P. 1939. *The Cuckoo* (Cuculus canorus). Witley [Privately printed].

Chance, Edgar P. 1940. *The Truth About the Cuckoo*. London, Country Life Ltd.

Compton, Piers. 1973. *The Story of Bisham Abbey*. Maidenhead, Thames Valley Press.

Cookham Dean Church. [Folder with map SU88(41/88) in Maidenhead Public Library, Local History Dept.]

Cookham Rural District Council. 1895–1934. *Minutes* [Held by Berkshire Record Office, Reading].

Darby, Stephen. 1890. *Notebooks on the History of Cookham*, [Handwritten] 18 vols. [In: Maidenhead Public Library, Local Collection].

Darby, Stephen. 1909. *Chapters in the History of Cookham*, Berkshire [Privately printed].

Darby, Stephen. 1899. *Place and Field Names, Cookham Parish* [For private circulation].

Dodds, M. Helen. 1954. *The Royal Manor of Cookham* [Handwritten, unpublished] Cookham Dean.

Domesday. 1988. *The Berkshire Domesday*. 3 vols. London, Alecto Historical Editions.

Duchess of Cleveland. 1889. *The Battle Abbey Roll with Some Account of the Norman Lineages by the Duchess of Cleveland* in 3 volumes. London, John Murray [*Pinkenie* Vol. 3, pp.8–9].

Dugdale, William. 1817. *Monasticum anglicanum: a history of the abbies and other monasteries, hospitals, friaries and cathedral and collegiate churches, with their dependencies, in England and Wales, also all such Scotch, Irish and French monasteries, as were in any manner connected with religious houses in England* [Originally published in Latin].

Gough, Richard. 1814. *A catalogue of the books relating to British topography and Saxon and Northern literature bequeathed to the Bodleian Library in the year MDCCXCIX by Richard Gough/ [by] Bodleian Library et al.* 1814. Oxford, Clarendon Press. 459 pp.

Holinshed, R. 1577. *Chronicles of England, Scotlande and Irelande; conteyning, the description and chronicles of England, from the first inhabiting unto the conquest.* London.

Hudson, W.J. 1919. *Birds in Town and Village.* London, Dent.

Kerr, R.G. 1932. *The Story of the Girl Guides.* London, Girl Guides Association.

Kerry, Charles. 1861. *The History and Antiquities of the Hundred of Bray, in the County of Berks.* By Charles Kerry, Master of the Bray and Holyport School. Printed for the author by Savill & Edwards, London.

Knibbs, Ray. 1989. *Furze Platt Remembered: A Personal History.* (Sweet, Herbert and Over, Luke eds.) Maidenhead, Clivedon Press.

Lacey, Paul. 1990. *Thames Valley. The British Years 1915–1920.* Paul Lacey.

Lacey, Paul. 1995. A *history of Thames Valley Traction Company 1920–1930.* Paul Lacey.

Lacey, Paul. 2005. *Was Grandma on the Buses? Family Tree Magazine.* 21 (8): 5–7.

Leland, John. 1544. *The Itinary of John Leland the Antiquary.* 2nd edn. Oxford [travelled in 1530s and 1540s].

Leland, John. 1549. *The Laboryouse Journey and Serche of J. Leylande for Englandes Antiquities, Given of Hym as a Newe Yeares Gyfte to King Henry the VIII* [Original in Bodleian Library, Oxford].

Maidenhead Advertiser (Over, Luke). 1997. *Images of Maidenhead.* Maidenhead Advertiser. Derby, Breedon Books Publishing Company.

Nairn, J. A. 1948. *Stubbings Parish Church Magazine.* October.

Nairn, J. A. 1950. *St. James the Less, Stubbings, 1849–1950. A Record by the Revd. J.A. Nairn, Vicar.* Centenary Number. January 1950. 2nd edn. Maidenhead, W. H. Marsh.

National Trust. 1979. *The Greens and Commons of Maidenhead and Cookham owned by the National Trust.* (Fearon, Henry, Ed.).

Natural History Museum. 2002. *Letters to Mary S. Peacock,* October.

Over, Luke. 1984. *The Story of Maidenhead*. Newbury, Local Heritage Books.

Over, Luke. 1986. *Domesday Revisited*. Windsor, Maidenhead and East Berkshire. Maidenhead, Thames Valley Booksellers.

Over, Luke and Tyrell, C. 1994. *The Royal Hundred of Cookham*. Maidenhead, Cliveden Press.

Palgrave, Francis. 1827. *The Parliamentary writs and writs of military summons, together with the records and Muniments relating to the suit and service due and performed to the King's High Court of Parliament and the Councils of the Realm, or affording evidence of attendance given at parliaments and councils.* Collected and edited by Francis Palgrave, Esq. FRS and FSA of the Honourable Society of the Inner Temple, Barister at Law. Vol. 1 Printed by Command of His Majesty King George IV in pursuance of an address of the House of Commons of Great Britain.

Peacock, Mary S. 2001 (reprinted 2009). *Grandfather's Samplers and the Peacock Tree*. Romsey, Village and Family History Project.

Peacock, Mary S. 2009. *Pinkneys Green – A History*. Othery, SDH Publishing.

Pinkney Family. 1920. *The History of the Pinkney Family* [Typescript]. [Document 4427 in Wiltshire Record Office, Trowbridge].

Pinkneys Green Scouts. 1987. *P.G. Revisited. A Walk New Years Day 1987 AD. 'Gryphon'*. Pinkneys Green Scouts.

Rocque, John. 1761. *A Topographical Survey of the County of Berks in 18 sheets*.

Steele, Edward. 1718. *Catalogue of books bequeathed to the Bodleian by R. Gough, 1814 No. 24 Collections for the County of Berks by Edw. Steele, 1718 Being a description of each funeral monument in the Church of Cookham in County Berks with their respective inscription and coats of Arms.*

Tomalin, R.W. 1919. *H. Hudson: A Biography*. London, Faber.

Victoria County History. 1972. *Berkshire*. Vol. 3 p.127.

Walker, E.W. 1936. *Ainley Skrine of Warleigh* [Privately printed].

Walker, R.E. 1973. *Pinkneys Green and the Village Cricket Club*. Maidenhead. Maidenhead Advertiser Printing Service.

Whately, Thomas. *Mr. Whately's Book*. Rev. Thomas Whately, [Vicar of Holy Trinity Church, Cookham 1797–1837]. Document DP/43/28/9 in Berkshire Record Office, Reading.